01

The Curious History of God

THE CURIOUS HISTORY OF GOD

RUSSELL STANNARD

Illustrations by
Taffy Davies

Text copyright © 1998 Russell Stannard
Illustrations copyright © 1998 Taffy Davies
This edition copyright © 1998 Lion Publishing

The author asserts the moral right
to be identified as the author of this work

Published by
Lion Publishing plc
Sandy Lane West, Oxford, England
ISBN 0 7459 3964 3

First edition 1998
10 9 8 7 6 5 4 3 2 1 0

Typeset in Candida

Printed and bound in Great Britain
by Biddles Ltd, Guildford and King's Lynn

Contents

What this book is about

◆ If there is only one God, why does the Bible sometimes talk as though there were lots of them?

◆ If God is the God of the whole world, why did he live up a mountain in the desert?

◆ If God loves little children, how come he killed off the Egyptians' first-born children?

◆ If God is the God of all peoples, why did he drown the Egyptian army (those poor Egyptians again)?

◆ If God is supposed to be so loving and forgiving, why did he fly into terrible tempers and threaten to wipe out the whole human race?

These are just some of the questions I used to ask as a boy. I liked reading the Bible (well, bits of it), but much of it didn't seem to make sense.

It was only when I grew up that I discovered what was going on. In the same way as people's understanding of the world has changed and improved over time (through science), so their ideas and understanding of God have changed and developed.

The stories of the Bible were written by different people living in different ages. So, it is hardly surprising that the picture we get of God in one part can seem different from that in another.

In this book, I retell some of those stories. I do so in a way that shows how people, over the course of history, gradually came to know God better.

Russell Stannard

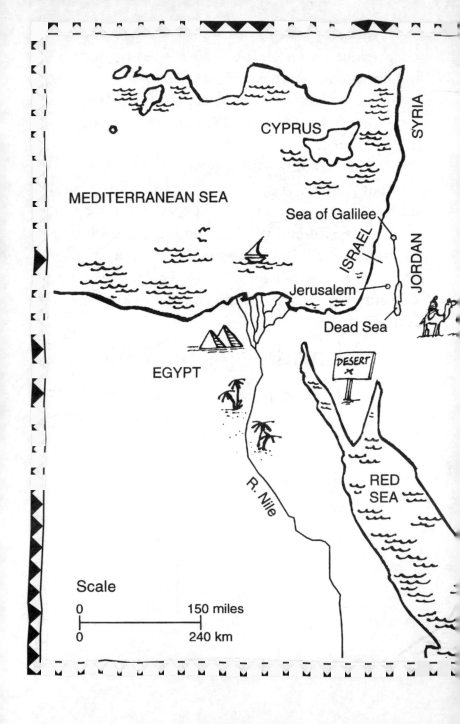

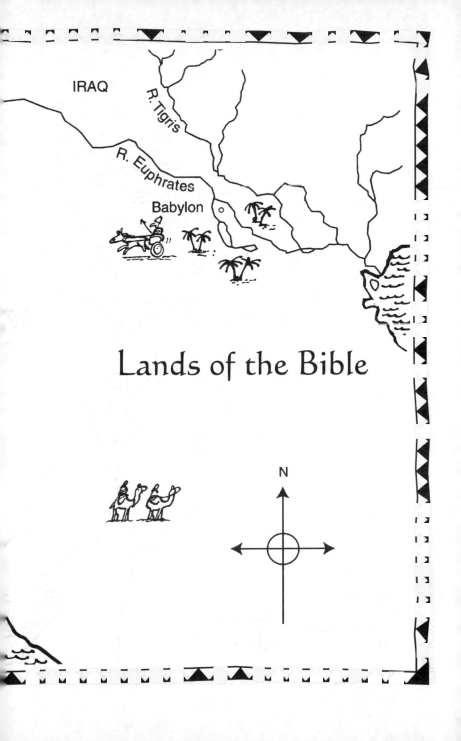

IRAQ

R. Tigris

R. Euphrates

Babylon

Lands of the Bible

N

Greedy gods

Long, long ago, people believed the world was ruled by gods. There were lots of them. They were cruel, fierce, and blood-thirsty.

Each was in charge of a particular country or stretch of land. Everyone living there had to worship that god. The same went for visitors. As they crossed the border from one country to the next, they had to forget the previous god, and start

worshipping the one who ruled the country they had now entered. That meant bowing down before statues of gold, or stone, or wood. The gods might be in the form of animals or of humans; sometimes they were half-animal and half-human.

And it was not enough to kneel before them and tell them how great, how wonderful they were. The gods were hungry. They were always needing to be fed. Every day the people had to make sacrifices on an altar, killing their very best animals. They even had to slaughter human beings. They tried to get away with just killing criminals and prisoners captured in war — people they did not really care about. But often this did not work; the gods were greedy. They demanded that every family sacrifice their eldest child. Mothers and fathers had to hand over their children to be killed. They did not dare to disobey.

The gods did whatever they liked. Sometimes they would look after their people; more often they wouldn't. You could never trust the gods; they were always changing their minds. You could

never be sure of pleasing them. So it was that
people lived in constant fear of their savage gods.

Moses meets the mountain god

One day, about 3,000 years ago, a man named
Moses had the shock of his life. He met one of the
gods. He was looking after a flock of sheep at the
time, and some had strayed up a mountain slope.
This could have spelt big trouble for Moses
because the god who owned this mountain did
not like people trespassing on his land. Usually,
you only had to put one foot on his mountain and
that was that — you were dead! But for some
reason, he let Moses off.

Though we say he 'met' the god, it wasn't like
coming face to face with someone. What Moses
actually saw was a bush. It was on fire — a mass
of flames — and yet the twigs and leaves of the
bush didn't seem to be getting burnt up. As you'd
expect, Moses was puzzled by this. He went to
take a closer look. Immediately there came a
voice — out of the bush! 'Don't come any closer!'
it commanded. It was the god of the mountain.
Moses stopped dead in his tracks.

The god said he was the god of the Israelites
— the nation to which Moses belonged. But that
was odd, thought Moses. The Israelites did not
live up this mountain. They were miles away in
Egypt. They were a poor down-trodden people
who had been slaves to the Egyptians for the past
400 years. The only reason Moses wasn't there
with them was that he had managed to escape.

Besides, Moses knew all about the 'god of the
Israelites'. Since he was a child, he had heard how
the founder of their nation, Abraham, had met
their god and sat and eaten with him. Abraham's

grandson Jacob had once had a wrestling match with him. (He had then had his name changed to Israel, meaning 'he struggles with God'.) The god liked walking in his garden in the cool of the evening. He had promised Abraham he would always look after his nation (not that this was working out very well; the Israelites were an unruly lot and had landed up as common slaves). How could *that* god have anything to do with this mountain god — this god who was invisible, spoke through the crackle of fire, and wouldn't let you get near him?

Moses was confused. He wanted to be sure who the god was. 'What's your name?' he asked.

'I am who I am,' the god replied. Which was a funny way of saying that Moses and the Israelites would have to wait and see. They would find out who he was through what he was going to do with them. Because his name seemed so special, the Israelites decided to call him simply 'the Lord'.

SMALL ADS.

THE LATEST IN CENTRAL HEATING

THE BURNING BUSH THAT NEVER GOES OUT!

The Lord then told Moses to go back to Egypt and tell the king that he had to set the Israelites free. Moses was to lead his people out of Egypt. The Lord promised to take them to a wonderful land that would be all their own.

'Some hope!' thought Moses. 'Why would a king listen to the likes of *me* — a mere shepherd?!'

But the Lord told him it would be all right. He himself was going to strike the Egyptians down. 'How's he going to do that?' Moses must have wondered. 'He belongs up here on this mountain. He can't just do as he likes in some other country — a country ruled by another god!'

Escape from Egypt

But Moses was wrong. When the king refused to listen to him, the Egyptians didn't know what had hit them. First, there was a plague of frogs, then gnats, then flies. The Egyptian cattle were dying, their people got terrible spots all over their bodies, and giant hailstones flattened their crops and killed farm animals as they stood in the fields. Then came locusts — insects that covered the ground and ate up the remains of the crops left after the hailstorm.

But the worst was still to come. The Lord showed what a terrifying god he was by killing the eldest child of every Egyptian family, including the eldest son of the king. The Egyptians woke up one morning to find that there was not a single house without

someone dead in it. And yet none of the Israelites had died. These dreadful disasters never harmed the Israelite slaves. This is how the Lord showed that he not only had power to do things on his own special mountain, but he could also do whatever he wanted in a country belonging to another god. In this way he was not like other gods.

The death of so many of their children was the final straw for the Egyptians. They decided to let the Israelites go free. Moses led his people out of Egypt.

But no sooner had they left than the Egyptians began to have second thoughts. With their slaves gone, who was going to do all the hard work? They changed their minds. They sent their army after the Israelites to bring them back. The fleeing Israelites got as far as the sea, but now their way was blocked. No problem. The Lord pushed the waters apart to let them through to the other side.

The chasing Egyptians followed. But when they were halfway across, the Lord made the sea sweep down on them and every single soldier was drowned.

This escape, or exit, from Egypt — now called the Exodus — became the most famous event in the whole history of the Israelites. It is still remembered and celebrated today by their descendants, the Jews. It showed Moses that the Lord was truly on the side of his people.

An agreement

Once the Israelites had got away from the Egyptians, Moses took them to meet their god on his special mountain. But when they got there, only he was allowed to climb up through the clouds to the top; the rest were warned to stay clear (if not, they would be struck dead!). There was thunder and lightning. The whole mountain shook, and fire and smoke burst out of the top. The people were terrified. The Lord was talking to Moses.

When he came down, Moses was carrying two blocks of stone with writing carved on them. The Lord had told Moses he would continue to be the Israelites' god and look after them. But, in return, they had to do what *he* commanded. They were to agree to live their life the way *he* wanted. The writing on the stone blocks spelt out how they had to behave. These were the Lord's 'Ten Commandments'. They said how the Israelites were to live: they had to tell the truth; they were not to commit murder, or steal, or swear, or make eyes at other people's husbands and wives, or be jealous of what their neighbour had. They had at all times to be respectful to the Lord and — most importantly — they had to love him and never, never worship any of the other gods. It didn't matter which country they were in; they had to carry on loving and worshipping him and *only* him.

Which was difficult. How could you be expected to worship a god you were never allowed to see — an invisible god? Even Moses himself was not allowed to look on the face of their god. The Lord had told Moses that such a sight would be so awesome and tremendous, the shock of it would kill him straight away. No, it was going to be hard. In fact, even in the short time Moses had been up the mountain, getting his orders from the Lord, the people had already made a new god for themselves — a golden statue of a calf! They were dancing around it and singing its praises when

Moses arrived back. He flew into a rage. He was so mad, he slammed the stone blocks down and broke them. As for the Lord himself, he was *furious*! His anger knew no bounds. He was all set to kill the lot of them. But Moses threw himself flat on

the ground, and begged him not to do it. To everyone's relief, the Lord listened to Moses. He decided to give them a second chance.

So it was that the Israelites agreed that in future they would do as they were told. They didn't really have much alternative. After all, he had already brought them out of slavery, so they owed everything to him.

IT IS HEREBY AGREED BY THE FOLLOWING PARTIES
- SIGNATURES:-

THE LORD ....

THE ISRAELITES...........

DATE............

It was a strange sort of relationship. Usually, people worshipped the god in charge of the country where they happened to have been born. There was no choice in the matter. It was a bit like being born — when you don't have any say over who your father and mother are. Now one of the gods had *chosen* a nation to be his people; and they had entered into an agreement.

Off to the promised land

Having left their homes in Egypt behind, where were the Israelites going to live now?

Many, many years before the Exodus, the Lord had promised the Israelite leader, Abraham, that one day his people would live in a wonderful country that would be all their own. He was now going to keep his word. He wasn't like the other gods; this one you could *trust*.

But that was odd. How could he lead his people to another country? Didn't he belong to this mountain stuck out in the desert? Gods were supposed to stay where they were and watch over their own territory.

Again this god was different. As the Israelites journeyed, the Lord went with them. He really was their very own god.

After spending a long time wandering through the hot desert, they eventually reached a country called Canaan. (It's at the Eastern end of the Mediterranean Sea.) This was their 'promised land'. It looked fertile and fabulous! The trouble was that it was already occupied — by Canaanites — and it belonged to other gods called 'Baals'.

No problem. The Israelites went to war. After many years of fighting with the Canaanites, the Israelites finally won and took over the land. They smashed up all the altars of the Baals, and Canaan became the new territory of *their* god — the Lord.

As for Moses, he was delighted to see the promised land after all their wanderings. But he only ever got to see it from a distance. He was an old man now, and he died before he got the chance to enter it. (Which was a pity.) As he

lay on his bed dying, he told the people of a new promise the Lord had made: one day they would get a new leader just like himself. The Israelites thought, 'Great! He will lead us to final victory over all our enemies.' Later, they were to call him the 'Messiah' and they longed for the day when he would come.

The kings of Israel

In those days, most countries were ruled by kings. But the Israelites were different; they were ruled by wise judges. This was because they regarded the Lord as their king, and they thought it would not be right to have an earthly king as well as a heavenly one.

But this didn't last long. 'Why can't we have a proper king like everyone else?' the people grumbled. So they chose Saul to be their first king.

It was not a good choice. Saul always did what he wanted to do — not what the Lord told him he ought to be doing. The Lord got very angry with him. He decided that if the Israelites wanted a king, fair enough. But he would not allow the kingship to be passed on to any of Saul's family. He himself would decide who the next king was to be. To everyone's surprise, the Lord chose a shepherd boy, David, to be the future ruler.

David was a brave lad. When the Israelites were fighting their enemies, the Philistines, he volunteered to take on single-handed the Philistine's champion soldier — a huge man named Goliath. Goliath was so strong and power-ful that everyone was scared rigid by him — but not David. It was to be a fight to the death. Goliath was armed to the teeth, while David had just a few stones and a sling (a kind of catapult). And yet David won!

He immediately became the people's hero, and they couldn't wait for him to take over from Saul. King Saul didn't like this. He became extremely jealous of David's popularity. So much so, he tried to have him murdered — several times. But his plans failed. In the end, Saul killed himself after losing a battle. That was how David at last became king.

He turned out to be the most important king the Israelites were ever to have. Under his rule, Israel became a powerful, united nation. He made Jerusalem into a great city. He was a very religious man and loved the Lord so much he was always making up

hymns. These songs were so good, people still sing them today. (You can find them in the Bible in the book of Psalms.) King David was to become the most famous ancestor of Jesus.

Which does not mean he was perfect — far from it. He once fell in love with a woman who was already married. Her husband was a soldier in the army. King David got to wondering how he could get rid of him. He hit on a plan. He arranged for the man to be placed in the front line of battle where the fighting was most dangerous — where the chances of getting killed were greatest. Sure enough, just as David had hoped, the poor fellow did get killed. That left the way open for the king to take his widow. It was *not* how kings should behave. Afterwards he was very sorry for what he had done.

Things go badly wrong

On the death of King David, it was the turn of his son Solomon to become king. Solomon's reign got off to a good start. It marked a period when the Israelites were at peace with their neighbours.

He decided this was the time to build a temple in honour of the Lord. He built it in the capital city of Jerusalem. And what a temple it turned out to be! It was one of the great wonders of the world.

The inside of it — walls, ceiling, and even the floor — was covered in pure gold.

At the grand opening of the temple, the king stood before the altar with all the people and declared, 'O Lord God of Israel, there is no god like you in heaven above or on earth below.' They then sacrificed 22,000 cattle and 120,000 sheep and goats to show just how much they thought of him.

But there was a problem. King Solomon had lots of wives — 700 of them. (That in itself was all right, because it was allowed in those days.) The trouble was that some of his wives came from foreign countries. The Lord had already warned his people not to marry foreigners. He was worried that if they did, they might be tempted to worship the gods of the

foreigners rather than himself. And that's exactly what happened; some of Solomon's wives wanted to worship their own gods — even though they were now living in the country ruled by the Lord. Solomon, who was getting old by then, made a bad mistake: he gave in to their wishes, and had altars built to the foreign gods. He even allowed these other gods to be worshipped in the Lord's very own temple.

He had gone too far. The jealous Lord was angry with Solomon and his people for letting this happen. They had to be punished. So, he saw to it that the Israelites began to argue and fight among themselves. The once peaceful, united nation was split into two. Those who lived in the north carried on calling themselves 'Israel' and made a new king for themselves. Those in the south, near Jerusalem, took the name of another tribal leader

'Judah'. And all because they had not stuck by the agreement — the agreement they had made with the Lord that they would worship him, and only him.

Things get even worse

Soon after the Israelites first took over the promised land, they began to give up their old way of life. No longer did they roam the desert with their herds and flocks. Instead, they settled down with their own piece of land, and became farmers. They learned how to plant crops, because they knew

that they would still be there in the same place later in the year to collect the harvest.

They quickly discovered that crops needed to

be watered; if they weren't, they would dry up and
die. No rain, and the people would starve to death.
So they had better pray for rain. But whom should
they pray to? The Lord? That didn't seem a good
idea. The Lord was great when it came to fighting
battles and destroying their enemies with plagues;
he had proved that in Egypt, and in the way he
had defeated the Canaanites. He was a god of war.
But what did such a god know about *farming*?
After all, hadn't he lived all his life at the top of
a bleak mountain in the middle of the desert!?
Sure enough he had seen to it that during their
wanderings through the desert before they came
to the promised land, they had not starved, and he
had shown them where to find water. But when it
came to growing crops, it seemed a better plan to

pray to the experts — the gods who knew all about making rain — the gods of the Canaanites.

So it was that when the Israelites thought the Lord wasn't looking, they secretly began rebuilding altars to the old Baals. That's how worship of the Baals began all over again. So it wasn't just King Solomon and his foreign wives who were breaking the agreement with the Lord; everybody was at it.

Prophets to the rescue

Well, not quite *everybody*. There were some who never lost sight of their promise to the Lord. Among them were a few who were specially chosen by the Lord to pass on his messages to the people — like Moses had done long ago. These were to be called 'prophets'. They had to explain to the people what the Lord wanted them to do. Having done that, the prophets next had to explain to the Lord, on behalf of the people, how sorry they all were whenever they made a hash of things.

Most of the prophets never wanted to be prophets in the first place. It meant having to speak up in front of lots of people, sometimes before the king, sometimes before the priests of the temple. 'I'm not very good at that sort of thing,' they would complain to the Lord. 'Can't you send someone else instead? I'm sure they'd do a much better job…' It was a lonely life being a prophet, and it often got you into trouble.

But it was no good arguing. Once you had

been chosen, you had to go through with it. The reason was that although these people *thought* they were ordinary, they *weren't*. They were especially close to the Lord; they understood him. The Lord knew he would be able to use them, and their own particular experience of life, to reveal to others something of *himself*, and what he was *really* like.

So it was that with the Israelites getting more and more disobedient and forgetful of what they had promised to him, the Lord decided it was time to send in the prophets…

The rainmaker

One of the prophets was a fearsome-looking character called Elijah. He wandered through the country wearing a rough, hairy coat and leather shorts. At one time, he depended on birds to bring him bits of food to eat. If it hadn't been for them, he would have starved! What a way to live!

Elijah had to tell Ahab, the king of Israel, and his wife Jezebel, how angry the Lord was with them. The trouble was that Jezebel was a foreigner, and had been getting everyone, including the king, to worship *her* god — one of the Baals. Because she was a powerful queen and would stop at nothing, she began killing the priests who were loyal to the Lord. In this she was helped by the 450 priests of Baal she had set up throughout the country. If this mass murder was allowed to go on much longer, there would soon be no priests of the Lord left. Elijah had to act quickly. He persuaded the king to assemble all the priests of Baal together at one place at the same time. When this was done, Elijah stirred up the

crowd against them. The priests of Baal were
seized and marched off to a valley. There Elijah
ordered every single one of them to be killed.

And it wasn't just the king and queen Elijah
told off. He went about raging at the people as
well for not being loyal to the Lord. It was the
middle of a long dry spell, and the crops were
dying, and the people were praying to the Baals
for rain.

'Forget the Baals. Pray to the Lord instead,'
demanded Elijah.

'Much good that will do us,' muttered the
people. So, Elijah decided to challenge the Baals

to a competition. He went up a nearby mountain.
Bending down, and putting his head between his
knees, he prayed. He prayed really, really hard.
At first nothing happened. But then a tiny cloud
appeared; it grew and grew. As it did, it got
blacker and blacker. After a while, it covered the
sky. Then it rained cats and dogs; it came down in
torrents!

As you can imagine, the people were pretty
impressed by this. Elijah had shown them that the
Lord was not only a god of war, but he was also
a god who could make the crops grow; he could
look after his people's needs in peacetime as well
as lead them in war. There was no need for the
farmers to pray to the old Canaanite Baals. They
had only to ask the Lord.

And another thing: the Lord made clouds in the sky. That meant he was not only the god of the land of the Israelites, he must also be the god of the sky. And, as everyone knows, the sky stretches *everywhere*. That must be why the Lord could do great things anywhere he liked — not just on his mountain, or just in Canaan. That was how he was able to deal with the Egyptians. What a powerful god this god of the Israelites was turning out to be!

The wild man versus the wicked queen

But Elijah now found himself in deep trouble.
As you can imagine, Queen Jezebel was furious
to learn that all her priests had been executed.
She swore she would get Elijah for this. He was
to be hunted down and put to death. Elijah took to
his heels and fled to the desert. 'I've had enough,
Lord,' he moaned. 'Just let me die here.' (I said it
was no fun being a prophet.)

But he didn't die. Instead, after many days, he found himself on the same mountain where Moses had met the Lord all those years before. Just as it had been with Moses, there was a great and powerful storm; the wind raged, the mountain shook and fire belched out from the top of the mountain. When this had happened before, the Israelites, waiting at the bottom, had thought that all that noise was the voice of the Lord speaking to Moses. But Elijah realized it wasn't that at all. The Lord spoke to him on the mountain all right, but his voice was just a tiny whisper. In fact, it hardly made any sound at all. The Lord was speaking to him in the stillness. The *Lord's* thoughts were being quietly stirred up in *Elijah's* mind. And this was all done without a need for any sound outside at all!

SILENCE PLEASE

That was a wonderful discovery. Ever since then, people have learned how to listen for the voice of the Lord. It is not necessary to visit exploding volcanoes or to listen for the Lord's voice in the rumble of thunder. He can get through to someone even when they pray in silence.

(By the way, nasty Queen Jezebel was finally thrown out of the window of her palace by two servants. She fell to her death, and her body was eaten by dogs. I reckon it served her right.)

The man who loved his wayward wife

There was another prophet, Hosea. He was a very different sort of man to Elijah. He had a wife whom he loved dearly. But she caused him much unhappiness; she kept running off with other men.

In those days, the law was very strict about such things. If a wife was unfaithful to her husband, she was sentenced to death by stoning. (A crowd

49

would surround her, and hurl
rocks at her until she was
dead.)

But Hosea was a kind
man. He found that no
matter how badly his wife
behaved, he could not
stop loving her.
She had only to
say 'sorry', and his heart
would melt, and he would forgive her. He never
handed her over to the courts to be condemned
and stoned; he just kept taking her back.

And that, strange to say, is exactly how the
Lord felt about the people of Israel. Just as Hosea's
wife went after other men, so the Israelites kept
going after other gods, even though they had

promised to keep themselves only for him. The Lord knew that strictly speaking he ought to destroy them for being so wayward. But, for some reason, he couldn't bring himself to do it. Why?

Hosea knew the answer. He was the first to realize that the Lord must actually *love* his badly-behaved people — just as he himself couldn't help loving his badly-behaved wife. The agreement made with Moses was not a cold, legal, 'I'll-do-this-for-you-if-you'll-do-that-for-me' sort of arrangement. It was more like a marriage agreement — one based on love. And, just as Hosea was able to forgive his wife, he understood that the Lord could forgive his people. All they had to do was to say 'sorry', and then try to do better in the future.

That was the message the Lord now wanted one of his prophets to get across to his people. And he chose Hosea. Hosea knew, from his own experience, what forgiveness was all about.

Down with the rich!
Up with the poor!

When the Israelites first took up farming, some were more successful at it than others. They bought land, then more land. They hired servants, then more servants. Their flocks of sheep and herds of cattle grew. Their vineyards provided a never-ending flow of wine. They built enormous stone mansions to live in and to show off their wealth. Every week they held magnificent feasts for their friends, no expense spared.

The fact that most of the people were desperately poor didn't bother them in the slightest. They forced people to work for hardly any wages. They made sure that they kept most of the crops themselves, even though this left the children of the poor to go hungry. They simply didn't care what other people thought.

As for the Lord, they reckoned that as long as they gave him a share in the takings — through making sacrifices to him in the temple — he would be perfectly happy with the way things were. Killing animals on the altar was their way of giving presents to their god — either to show their gratitude to him for all he had done for them, or to make it up to him if they had done something wrong. (Often the sacrifices were a sham. Having slaughtered lots of animals, the people thought it would be a waste to throw all that meat away. So they cooked it and ate it instead. In other words, the 'sacrifices' were just an excuse to have another party!)

No one had the courage to speak up and say how unfair all this was. They feared that if they said anything, they and their children would be left with nothing at all — and would starve to death.

But then someone *did* begin to speak up. A voice was heard in the temples declaring, 'You are trampling on the poor! You are taking their food! You are denying them justice!'

Who was it? No one recognized him. Little wonder; he was just a poor shepherd from the south. His name was Amos. Everyone was amazed at him being daring enough to make such a commotion. But Amos had no choice.

The Lord had told him to leave his flocks and go to the northern part of the country and tell the rich rulers of the land that their god was angry with them; the Lord was horrified at the way so many of his people were suffering through the greed of the lucky few. If the rich thought they could get away with it by making sacrifices to him, they had better think again. Sacrifices were no protection against his anger. Unless they mended their ways, he would see to it that an enemy would invade their country, kill their king, and take all their wealth from them.

Again, the Lord was revealing something of what he was really like. He had already shown how he was on the side of the underdog nation (the Israelites) against the big bully nation (the Egyptians). But now he wanted to show that he was interested not just in the rights of *nations*; he also cared for the rights of *individual people* — the downtrodden poor rather than the uncaring rich. To get this message across, the Lord had to use someone who knew — from personal experience — what it was like to be poor and hungry. That was why he had picked this unknown shepherd to be a prophet.

But the rich refused to listen to Amos. They saw no reason to change their ways. So what Amos predicted came true. A few years after he had given his message, the Assyrian nation invaded the northern half of the country (Israel), the king was killed, and the wealth of the rich was taken from them. Two hundred years after the Israelite people had split in two, the northern half now ceased to exist as a separate nation. All that was left was the southern half: Judah.

Top god

While Hosea and Amos had been at work in Israel, there arose yet another prophet, this time in Judah. His name was Isaiah. What was *his* special message from the Lord?

Unlike Amos, he was one of the rulers. (But he wasn't like the other rich people; he cared greatly about the needs of the poor.) He spent much of his time in the court of the King of Judah. He knew all about the splendour of palaces, the power of kings, and how it was their job to rule their nations wisely. Perhaps this is why the Lord chose to reveal to Isaiah something of his *own* splendour. Isaiah had this vision — a kind of dream — where he saw the Lord in heaven as a great king, and his glory filling the whole earth.

'The *whole* earth' — not just the land of Judah. What did that mean? The Israelites already knew that the Lord could act in countries that were not his own. (He was the god of the sky, remember?) But this vision seemed to mean that the Lord actually *ruled* the whole earth — that he was in charge of *everything*! He was 'Number 1' — the world's TOP GOD!

And that was not all. The Lord told Isaiah how upset he was that the people still did not

seem to understand him. Take sacrifices, for example. All those animals being killed. Why?

'What are they to me?' declared the Lord. 'I have no pleasure in the blood of bulls and lambs and goats. Stop bringing meaningless offerings!'

No, what the Lord wanted was a people who lived good lives. That was what mattered. It was no good being selfish and cruel, and then thinking you could pay for it by killing a few animals on an altar. Making sacrifices for someone you genuinely love was fine — but not if it was all pretence and showing off.

Like Amos, Isaiah warned the people of hard times to come. But he went on to say that they were not to lose heart. He reminded them that the 'Messiah' — the new leader promised to Moses — was still to come. He would be a prince of peace who would rule them wisely. All would then be well.

The king who tried to put things right

Jeremiah was the son of a priest. He was a gentle and kindly person. When the Lord called him to be a prophet, he begged to be let off. 'I am too young,' he protested. (He was in his early twenties at the time.) But it was no good. Like the prophets before him, he was to discover that if you arc called to do something for the Lord, you just have to get on with it.

Jeremiah's first task was similar to that of the earlier prophets: he had to call the people to stop worshipping other gods. One of the problems was that every town, village, and hill had an altar. This was where the sacrifices were made. That wasn't so bad. The trouble was that with each

town having its own altar, the people got to talking of 'the Lord of *our* town'. Those living down the road had *their* own altar, and *their* own Lord. In other words, they had slipped back into the bad old ways of worshipping local Baals all over again!

Fortunately for Jeremiah, he lived at a time when Judah was ruled by a good man, King Josiah. The king himself had decided to put a stop to all this worshipping of other gods — once and for all. He had a brainwave. He had all the altars smashed up — except one. That was the altar in the great temple at Jerusalem. From now on, he declared, anyone wanting to offer sacrifices to the Lord had to do it in this one place, or not at all.

It was a clever plan. At a stroke, it made the Israelites wake up to the fact that they really were supposed to worship just the one god. At first, Jeremiah was pleased with what the king had done. It seemed a smart move.

But then he had second thoughts. Perhaps concentrating worship in Jerusalem alone was not such a good idea after all. The trouble was that the people were beginning to think that Jerusalem was where the Lord actually lived. If you wanted to meet the Lord, you had to go up to Jerusalem to do it; you had to visit him in his temple because that was where he was. Of course, this meant that visits to Jerusalem were very, very special occasions. Which was fine. The problem came when the visit was over. As you left Jerusalem to go home, it felt as though you were leaving the

Lord behind too. So, for most of the year it seemed as though the Lord was miles away — he was in Jerusalem; you were in your own town.

This had not been what King Josiah intended at all. He had always tried to make it clear that the Lord still ruled the *whole* country. You could worship him at home as well as in Jerusalem.

BYE! SEE YOU NEXT YEAR!

But that was not how the people understood it. And not surprisingly, with the Lord out of the way (so they thought), the people began living their lives the way they wanted. Instead of obeying the commandments given to Moses, they took to crime, the poor were badly treated, and widows were left to starve.

Messenger in the mud

The Lord was angry. He told Jeremiah, 'My people have forgotten me. They are saying they are safe; that I shall never harm them.' The people had to learn that this was not the case. Jeremiah was to tell everyone, including the new king (good King Josiah having died) that they had better mend their ways. If they didn't, the Lord would punish them by getting their neighbours, the Babylonians, to attack them.

At first the crowds treated Jeremiah's warnings as a joke. They made fun of him and heaped insults upon him. Jeremiah hated it. He was a shy man. He swore to himself that in future he would keep quiet. But the Lord's words *burnt* inside him. Jeremiah found that, whether he liked it or not, he couldn't help speaking out.

He was reported to the rulers. The new king was furious. Who did this Jeremiah guy think he was, going round upsetting everyone with his wild tales of war and destruction? How dare he tell the king how he should be running the country? In no

time, Jeremiah, like Elijah before him, had to flee for his life and go into hiding.

He got caught. By way of punishment, he was lowered down into a deep well. At the bottom he sank into thick, smelly mud. And there he was left. No food, no water. In the end a friend was able to rescue him and pull him out. He was lucky to get out alive.

But what Jeremiah had prophesied came true. The Babylonians struck. They invaded Judah and captured Jerusalem. Worse still, they took away all the treasures of the temple, and burnt the place to the ground. After standing for 350 years, there was now nothing left of the great temple King Solomon had built.

As for the leaders and other important citizens of Judah, they were all carried off to Babylon as prisoners of war. So, first the northern half of the country, Israel, had been destroyed, and now the southern half, Judah, had gone the same way.

It was a disaster. It was like the end of the world for the Jewish people. Their nation had been swept away. As for their god, who could say what had become of him? For the last twenty or so years they had got

used to the idea that the Lord was to be found only in his temple. But now there was no temple. Their god had been made homeless, just like themselves. Or worse still, perhaps he had been destroyed along with the temple. The people were confused and sad; they did not know what to think.

Jeremiah was now given a new message to pass on to them. Instead of telling them off for their bad behaviour, as he had done in the past, he was to speak words of comfort. Jeremiah, unlike the rulers, had not been carried off to

Babylon, so he had to write them a letter from Judah. He explained how the Lord would continue to punish the people for their wickedness for the next seventy years. But after that, he would make sure that the Jews came back home. They would be given another chance. They would be able to make a fresh start. It was a message of hope for the future.

Jeremiah was also to tell them how the destruction of the temple was not that important. The Lord was not to be found in the ruins of Jerusalem; he was to be found in their *own hearts*. This was something Jeremiah had always known to be true in his own life. He was now sharing this understanding with others. He told them how the Lord was always with them — with each and every one — wherever they happened to be. The Lord filled the heavens and the earth. He could be worshipped at any time, in any place — even in Babylon. He would always hear them. There was no god like him. The Lord was not so much interested in nations, or countries, or buildings; he loved *individuals* — people just like you and me.

Madman or genius?

The prophet Ezekiel was a strange man. Some thought he was mad. Soon after he was taken prisoner to Babylon with the others, he had an absolutely wild, fantastic vision. It seemed as though there were great storm clouds and flashes of lightning and a fire of shining molten metal. In the centre of this fire there appeared to be creatures with four faces and four wings. On the ground beneath were wheels locked together. Above was a covering of sparkling ice, and above that a jewelled throne. On the throne sat a figure like that of a man. He glowed with fire and the brilliance of rainbows surrounded him. Ezekiel did not know what was happening to him, but knew that he must be in the presence of the Lord. So he threw himself to the ground.

This extraordinary experience left Ezekiel in a state of total shock. It lasted for seven days! When he recovered, he attempted to tell others about his vision; he tried to describe what he had seen. But deep down he knew he couldn't. There were no words — none at all — that could do justice to what he had seen and felt. All he knew was that he had seen a glimpse of just how powerful, awesome and wonderful the Lord really was. The Lord was greater than the entire world. He stretched beyond the limits of human imagination.

During the vision, he had heard the voice of the Lord. As with Jeremiah, Ezekiel was to tell the people that they had to mend their ways, but he was also to speak words of comfort to them. One day they would return to their homeland; their

nation would rise again. They were to take heart:
the Lord was watching over them as a shepherd
looking after his flock.

Mystery man

You might have thought that the many Jews now living in Babylon would have begun worshipping the victorious god of the Babylonians. But, with the encouragement of people like Jeremiah and Ezekiel, they did not. They continued to worship their own god.

Then, towards the end of their long exile in Babylon, one of the most important prophets of all time began his work. Nothing is known of him, except his teachings. These are to be found in the Bible, within the book of the prophecies of Isaiah. For this reason, he is known as 'Second Isaiah', although some simply call him 'Isaiah' (which can be a little confusing!).

The Lord told this mystery man, 'As the heavens are higher than the earth, so are my ways higher than your ways, and my thoughts than your thoughts.' This meant that mere humans could never really hope fully to understand the Lord — which is what Ezekiel had learned earlier from his vision.

Then came the most surprising of all the Lord's messages. Over the years, ever since the first Isaiah had had his unforgettable vision of the Lord ruling the whole world, there had seemed less and less for the other gods to do. They were pretty useless. Was there, in fact, anything *at all* left for them to do? Isaiah was now told to say:

'I am the Lord, and there is no other;
apart from me, there is no other god.'

That was the answer: there was only ONE GOD! The other gods had nothing to do because there *weren't* any other gods; the Baals had never even existed!

Straight away, everything began to make sense:

◆ Why had the Lord always made such a big fuss about the Israelites worshipping only him? It was because he didn't want his people wasting time and effort worshipping gods that weren't even there. From now on the Lord could simply be called 'God' — with a capital 'G' — because there were no other gods he could be confused with.

GOD MADE THIS... AND THIS... AND THIS... AND THIS... AND THIS...

◆ Why had he been able to leave his mountain and settle in another country? Because every place in heaven and on the earth belonged to him. He could live wherever he wanted. *He owned the lot!* And not only did he own it, God explained how he had *created* it all in the first place — the heavens, the earth, all peoples, and all living creatures.

◆ How had he been able to get the Egyptians to let the Israelites go free at the Exodus? Because he was the God of the Egyptians as well as the God of the Israelites. He was the God of *all* peoples. He had power over everyone. And if he could get the Israelites out of captivity in Egypt, he could get them out of Babylon one day.

The Lord was God of all peoples, and yet the Israelites were still special to him. It was to them that he had first shown his true nature. Now they had to pass that news on to the rest of the world. For this they would be given a rough time by the other nations — just as they had themselves made their own prophets suffer when they came with their messages from God. Isaiah described a 'suffering servant' who would bring justice to all the nations, but would be mocked for his loyalty to God. This servant was meant as a symbol of the Jewish nation as it carried God's messages to other nations. But was it also a prophecy that an *actual person* was still to come — someone who would suffer for the people? It was not clear.

Returning home

Talking of 'a person still to come', was it not time for the long-expected Messiah to arrive? Perhaps he would be the one to lead them back to their own country when the seventy-year exile was over. That was the hope.

Eventually the seventy years were up and the exile did come to an end. But it was not thanks to a Messiah. The Babylonians were defeated by another nation: the Persians. All the land that had belonged to Babylon (including Israel and Judah) now became part of the Persian Empire. Under the new rulers, the Jews were allowed to return home at last.

On arriving back at Jerusalem, in the year 520BC, they set to and rebuilt the temple. It was nothing like as grand as Solomon's first temple (they couldn't afford it). But it was still a great joy to the Jews.

AH...THEY CAN'T BUILD TEMPLES LIKE THEY USED TO IN THEM GOOD OLD DAYS!

And so it was that the Jews lived for 200 years under the rule of the Persians. Then they became part of another empire when the Persians in their turn were defeated by the Greeks. And after that, in 63BC, they became part of the Roman Empire.

In all this time, no further major prophets arose. The age of the great prophecies had come to an end. The people probably thought that this was because God had nothing more to reveal of

himself. They stopped looking out for prophets and simply got on with their lives.

But then, when least expected, there came a person so extraordinary, he outshone all who had gone before. He came from a humble background: his father was a carpenter. And he lived in a small, unimportant town. He was never rich; he did not lead armies into battle. And yet he was a descendant of the great King David. His name? Jesus.

The one who was to come

Almost everyone today has heard of Jesus. Two thousand years after his death, millions upon millions of people all over the world regard him as the greatest person who has ever lived. Why? What made him special?

First there were the things he said. He taught his followers to love God with all their heart. They could speak to God as their heavenly Father, because he was a kind, friendly, loving God who was always ready to listen. They also had to love each other. That didn't mean just loving your family and friends — that's easy. No, you had to love *everyone* — including even your *enemies*! No matter what they did to you, you must never try to get your own back on them; you were to forgive them instead. That was tough, but it is what he himself did, and he expected his followers to do the same. They had to see everyone as belonging to a great family — all brothers and sisters together, having the same heavenly Father.

He taught that we had to live a good life, keeping God's commandments. That was nothing new; the other prophets had been saying that. What *was* new was that Jesus said that we must not even *think* of doing bad things. Just to *think* it was as bad as actually *doing* it.

Now, you might think that this was asking too much. He wanted people to be perfect. Nobody could manage *that*! Except that that was exactly what Jesus was. He himself lived a perfect life. He never did anything wrong. He was always helping the poor, comforting the sad, and sticking up for those who were badly treated. He healed blind

people and
those who
could not
walk. He
mixed with
all sorts of
people —
not just the
important
ones. As for
children, he
thought the
world of them.

He told adults that if they wanted to see the
Kingdom of God, they had better become like
children — it wasn't the other way round. That
was one in the eye for the adults!

His perfect life was the second thing that
made him special. It was the first and only time
anyone had managed it.

Now, you might think
everyone would have
wanted to be friends
with such a wonderful
person. Some did. He
gathered around him
twelve special friends
who left their homes

and jobs and followed him everywhere; they were
to be called Jesus' disciples. There were also
several women who were equally devoted to him.
But there were other people who were against
him. Strange to say, he had quite a lot of enemies.
Perhaps they were jealous, perhaps they thought
he was showing them up. Anyway, whatever the
reason, they had him arrested, tortured, and killed
in the most cruel way. He was nailed to a wooden
cross, and left to die in terrible pain. And yet,
Jesus never complained. As the nails were being
hammered into his hands and feet, he forgave
those who were doing it.

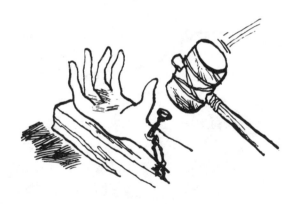

The one who came back

The way Jesus lived was unusual enough. But something even more amazing was to happen — the third reason why he was so special. Three days after he died, and his body was buried, he was seen alive again! God had raised him from the dead.

BURIAL CHAMBER FOR SALE
HARDLY USED

His friends were stunned. What did it mean? They had known all along he was the best man who had ever lived, but this showed he was even more than that. They came to realize that Jesus was none other than *God himself*! God had come to earth in the form of a human being!

Everything began to slot into place. As they looked back over his life, they saw that he himself had always known he was going to die that terrible death. He had let it happen to him, even though (being God) he could easily have stopped it. He had offered himself as a kind of sacrifice to show how much God loved his people — just as the Jews had always offered sacrifices in the temple to God to show how much they thought of him. Although Jesus himself had never done any wrong, he was prepared to pay the price for all the wrongdoing of others, so as to make things right again between God and his people.

The disciples saw that throughout his life he had been giving them hints and clues as to who he really was — like, for example, the way he had described himself as the 'Good Shepherd' (which, you remember was exactly how Ezekiel had described God). Then there was the time when his friends told him how they would like to see God — their heavenly Father. Jesus had replied that to have seen him — Jesus — was to have seen the Father.

It dawned on them that Jesus was not only God, but he was also the long awaited Messiah —

the Prince of Peace. The Messiah had come at last, and they hadn't even noticed! This was not surprising. They had been expecting a Messiah who would have been the champion of the Jewish people, their warrior prince. But Jesus had seemed to be an all-time loser — especially in the way he had died.

Not only that, but they now saw that Jesus was also the 'suffering servant' spoken of by Isaiah.

What happened next? During the few days the risen Jesus appeared to his friends, he could only, of course, be in one place at one time. But that was not good enough. In the years to follow — up to the present day — everyone all over the world was going to be needing his help, all at the same time. This would not be possible while he was still walking around on the earth as a human being. So Jesus stopped appearing to people in human form; he withdrew to heaven, and sent instead his Holy Spirit. This was God invisible, God *spread out everywhere*. This way he could be with all his friends, wherever they were, whenever they needed him. Those who followed him were to share his life; he was to share theirs.

The story of God — so far

You have now seen how God helped his people over the years to learn more and more about himself:

◆ Instead of him being one god among many others he was the *only* God — the single God who could be known as our Heavenly Father, as God in human form (Jesus), and as God the Holy Spirit.

◆ Instead of a god who lived only on a mountain, God is the Creator and Ruler of the whole world.

◆ Instead of a god who was interested only in the Israelites, he is the God of all people.

◆ Instead of a god who was always angry, jealous, and vengeful, he is just and loving.

◆ Instead of a god who seemed to think nothing of killing Egyptian children, we have Jesus saying, 'Let the children come to me'.

◆ Instead of a god who demanded sacrifices from people, Jesus allowed *himself* to be killed for others.

◆ Instead of a god who is only to be found far away in heaven, he is the God who became a human being, and who can live in people's hearts.

◆ Instead of a god to be frightened of, he is the God we respect and love.

It is not that God has changed over the years. God never changes. No, it is simply that we now understand much better what he is really like — and it took time for people to work that out. (You know how it is when you meet someone new. You form a first impression of them. But then as time goes on, and you get to know them, you gain a clearer idea as to who they truly are.)

All these different ideas about God are to be found in the Bible. The Bible is a wonderful collection of many writings, some very old, others more recent. Unfortunately these writings do not always appear in the order in which they were written. It takes a bit of detective work to sort out the right order. But now you know the story of how God has revealed himself over time, it should be a little easier for you to find your way around your Bible.

What next?

Before Jesus left to go to heaven, he told his friends he had more things to tell them. But he would leave it to the Holy Spirit (who was coming later) to lead them into 'all truth'. What did he mean by this?

He could have meant that there was yet *more* to learn about God, but for some reason, the people of that time were not ready for it.

OUR PARENT...
WHO ART IN HEAVEN...

For example, until quite recently, it was thought that men were much more important than women. All the top jobs went to men, and women got a very raw deal. This being so, it seemed only natural in the old days to think of God as masculine. But that is now changing. Now we recognize that in all the ways that matter, women are just as important as men. So, why should God be more like a man than a woman? Could it be that we are learning how God is just as much our heavenly Mother as our heavenly Father?

And what of other religions? This book has traced the manner in which *Christians* have come to understand God. Much of the path they have followed is common to that of the Jewish and Islamic religions. Can people of different faiths enrich still further their understanding of God's impact on human life by sharing insights gained by other religions?

Then there is our modern scientific knowledge. Astronomical telescopes, for instance, allow us to see far beyond the sun and its planets. They have shown us how absolutely vast the universe is — filled with billions of billions of other suns (the stars). God must have made all that as well. So, he is even greater and more powerful than we thought.

Could there be intelligent forms of life out there, living on planets going round those distant suns? It is quite possible. If this is so, God will be their God as well as ours. Has he visited them in *their* form, as he visited us in human form? If we ever meet up with space aliens, we shall have to ask them!

New stars and planets are always being born, so new kinds of life are probably coming into being all the time. This means that God did not finish his work of creation a long time ago. It was not a once-and-for-all effort. He is still creating today.

These are just some of the ways we might be learning still more about God. No doubt there are more surprises in store for us.

THE END?!?

About the author

Russell Stannard is a professor of physics. He has spent much of his life carrying out scientific experiments into the nature of matter, space and time, using the giant atom-smashing machine in Geneva, Switzerland.

A Christian and a lay reader in the Church of England, he often broadcasts on religious TV and radio programmes. In his spare time, he enjoys making large sculptures.

He writes books for children — both about science and religion. He is best known for his books about the now famous character, Uncle Albert, which have become best-sellers around the world.

He has four grown-up children, three step-children, ten grandchildren, one fluffy cat, three goldfish and about 40 frogs.

As well as receiving the Templeton UK Project Award in 1986 for his work in science and religion, Russell Stannard was given an OBE in 1998 for his services to physics and to the popularization of science.